Specific Skil

Word Families

Activity Pages and Easy-to-Play Learning Games for Introducing and Practicing Short- and Long-Vowel Phonograms

by
Leland Graham, Ph.D.
and
Anchor R. Shepherd, Ed.S.

illustrated by
Vanessa Countryman

-at

-ain

-oad

-et

-ig

Publisher
Key Education Publishing Company, LLC
Minneapolis, Minnesota

CONGRATULATIONS ON YOUR PURCHASE OF A KEY EDUCATION PRODUCT!

The editors at Key Education are former teachers who bring experience, enthusiasm, and quality to each and every product. Thousands of teachers have looked to the staff at Key Education for new and innovative resources to make their work more enjoyable and rewarding. We are committed to developing educational materials that will assist teachers in building a strong and developmentally appropriate curriculum for young children.

PLAN FOR GREAT TEACHING EXPERIENCES WHEN YOU USE EDUCATIONAL MATERIALS FROM KEY EDUCATION PUBLISHING COMPANY, LLC!

About the Authors

Dr. Leland Graham is a former college professor, principal, and teacher, who was twice voted "Outstanding Teacher of the Year." The author of 55 educational books, Dr. Graham is a popular speaker and workshop presenter throughout Georgia and the United States, as well as a presenter for NSSEA (National School Supply and Equipment Association). Thousands of teachers have benefited from his workshops on reading, math, and improving achievement scores.

Anchor R. "Bunny" Shepherd began her educational career in Fort Wayne, Indiana, with Head Start after earning a bachelor's degree at Indiana University. Following a move to Florida to teach kindergarten, she and her family relocated to Georgia, where she continued her education at the University of West Georgia, majoring in early childhood and administration and supervision. Her experiences as an educator include teacher of kindergarten through third-grade classes, infant/toddler evaluator, adult educator, administrator, and literacy coach.

Acknowledgments

The authors would like to acknowledge the assistance of the following educators: Diane LaPointe, Payton Muglia, and Charles Shepherd.

Credits

Authors: Leland Graham, Ph.D.
and Anchor R. Shepherd, Ed.S.
Publisher: Sherrill B. Flora
Illustrator: Vanessa Countryman
Editors: Debra Pressnall, Karen Seberg, Claude Chalk
Cover Design and Production: Annette Hollister-Papp
Page Design and Layout: Sharon Thompson and
Key Education Staff
Cover Photographs: © Comstock, © Shutterstock,
© Photo Disc, and © Able Stock

Key Education welcomes manuscripts and product ideas from teachers. For a copy of our submission guidelines, please send a self-addressed, stamped envelope to:

Key Education Publishing Company, LLC
Acquisitions Department
9601 Newton Avenue South
Minneapolis, Minnesota 55431

Copyright Notice

Standard Book Number: 978-1-602680-10-4
Specific Skills: Word Families
Copyright © 2008 by Key Education Publishing Company, LLC
Minneapolis, Minnesota 55431

Table of Contents

Introduction 4

Letter to Parents 5

Assessments:
Pretest/Posttest A.....................6
Pretest/Posttest B....................7

Activity Pages

The -an Word Family 8
More Short "a" Word Families 9
Write -an, -ap, and -at Words............10
The -et Word Family 11
More Short "e" Word Families 12
Write -ed, -en, and -et Words 13
The -ig Word Family 14
More Short "i" Word Families 15
Write -ig, -in, -ip, and -it Words 16
The -ot Word Family 17
More Short "o" Word Families 18
Write -ob, -og, -op, -ot, and
      -ox Words 19
The -ug Word Family 20
More Short "u" Word Families............21
Write -ub, -ug, -um, and -ut Words.....22
Say and Match: -ap, -at,
      and -op Words 23–24
Board Game: Read and Race!
Directions and Game Pieces 25–28
Rhyme to Match 29–30
The -ain Word Family 31
Find the Word Family....................32
The -ee Word Family....................33
The -eep, -eet, and -ent Families 34
The -ice and -ike Word Families.........35

Find the Word Family.....................36
The -ose and -one Word Families.......37
Fill In the Names........................38
Looking for Clues 39
Building -une and -ute Words............40
More Fill In the Names....................41
Match 'Em Up! 42
The -all Family Story.....................43
The -ug Word Family Puzzle 44
The -ack Family Story 45
More Match 'Em Up! 46
The -eet Word Family 47
The -ice Word Family 48
The -ose Word Family 49
The -ool Word Family 50
Sense or Nonsense?....................51
The -ug Family Story.....................52
The -and Word Family....................53
The -oy Word Family 54
The -ip Word Family 55
The -ick Family Story 56
More Sense or Nonsense? 57
The -eat Word Family Questions.........58
The -ip Word Family Puzzle.................59
A Jumbo -ing Word Find 60
Game Board: Sky High Reading Fun ..61

Answer Key 62–63

**Correlations to
NCTE/IRA Standards and
NAEYC/IRA Position
Statement** 64

Introduction

Meet the needs of various students with the Specific Skills series. Here at your fingertips is a collection of activities to introduce students, especially struggling learners, to the concept of word families and to help them gain mastery of letter patterns in words. The hands-on activities, puzzles, practice pages, and easy-to-play games inspire students to use word parts (phonograms) and context to decode new words. Also included in this reproducible resource book is a pretest/posttest that is formatted according to national standards.

Specific Skills: Word Families supports the NCTE (National Council of Teachers of English) and IRA (International Reading Association) Standards by offering materials that help students acquire literacy skills. The practice pages and games have been designed to introduce, recognize, and identify a variety of word families. These materials can be used as whole group lessons, as independent student work, in learning centers, and as at-home enrichment activities.

Read-Aloud Picture Books

Build awareness of word families by sharing picture books that have rhyming text. Listed below are just a few of the many titles that could be read aloud to students. Dr. Seuss books are also a wonderful resource for rhyming text. If a word wall is used in the classroom, be sure to display words for selected word families that are discovered by your students.

- *In the Small, Small Pond* by Denise Fleming (Henry Holt, 1993)

- *In the Tall, Tall Grass* by Denise Fleming (Henry Holt, 1991)

- *Is Your Mama a Llama?* by Deborah Guarino and illustrated by Steven Kellogg (Scholastic Inc., 1989)

- *Pigs, Pigs, Pigs!* by Lesléa Newman and illustrated by Erika Oller (Simon & Schuster Books for Young Readers, 2003)

- *Rub-a-Dub Sub* by Linda Ashman and illustrated by Jeff Mack (Harcourt, 2003)

- *What Time Is It, Mr. Crocodile?* by Judy Sierra and illustrated by Doug Cushman (Gulliver Books, 2004)

Dear Parent,

Over the course of several weeks, our class will be learning about word families (phonograms). The students will be completing activity sheets and participating in hands-on, fun activities to recognize many common word families. This skill is important because children can use this knowledge of word parts when decoding new words in stories.

Perhaps, you are thinking "What are word families?" Many single-syllable words have common endings known as *phonograms*. For example, when the words *cat*, *bat*, *hat*, *mat*, and *rat* are compared, all of these words end with the word part "at." Thus, they belong to the *-at* word family. Other common word families include *-ack*, *-ain*, *-ake*, *-ame*, *-an*, *-ank*, *-ap*, *-eat*, *-est*, *-ice*, *-ick*, *-ide*, *-in*, *-ing*, *-ink*, *-ip*, *-ock*, *-ook*, *-oom*, *-oon*, *-op*, *-ug*, *-unk*, and many more.

You may see some of the activity sheets in your child's homework folder. Please review the work with your child to become informed about which word families are being discussed. As you share a bedtime story each night, encourage and assist your child in listening for the different phonograms. Discuss the location of word families in a variety of words. Also, invite your child to think of other words that rhyme with the selected word family. They do not necessarily have to be real words; nonsense words are encouraged! This simple, playful exercise makes those word families memorable for your child. Whenever possible, locate picture books with rhyming text and encourage your child to find and compare the words on the pages to look for common word families. Dr. Seuss books are a wonderful resource for rhyming text.

Please help your child maintain a good attitude and self-confidence about the ability to recognize word families. This will promote an eagerness to read as well as the knowledge that we are all working together to achieve success!

Thank you so much for your time and assistance.

Sincerely,

Pretest/Posttest A

To the Teacher: Direct the child to cut out the word families along the dashed lines below. Then, have the child name each picture and glue the correct word family in the large box to finish the word. For additional testing after completing the activity, have the child tell you a word that rhymes with each picture.

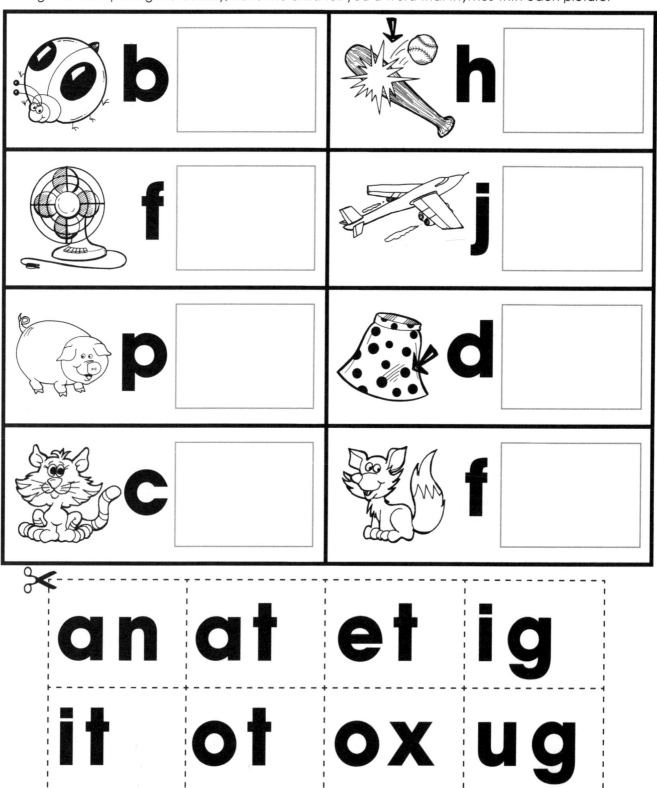

Pretest/Posttest B

To the Teacher: Direct the child to name each picture and then write the correct word family from the Word Family Bank on the line to complete the word. Remind the child to drawn an **X** in each box in the Word Family Bank when it is used. The child must write the entire word for each picture marked with a star. For additional testing after the activity, have the child tell you a word that rhymes with each picture.

p ____		h ____	
dr ____		c ____	
sn ____		b ____	
k ____		f ____	
★ ____		★ ____	

Word Family Bank

_ake	_eet	_um	_ace	_ing
_ole	_ool	_ed	_ose	_ube

The -*an* Word Family

Directions: Circle each picture whose name rhymes with **man**.

Something to Try! Write three words that rhyme with **man**.

_____   _____   _____

__can__   _____   _____

More Short "a" Word Families

Directions: Cut out the pictures below. Glue the pictures that rhyme in the same row. Write the letter for the sound at the **end** of the words.

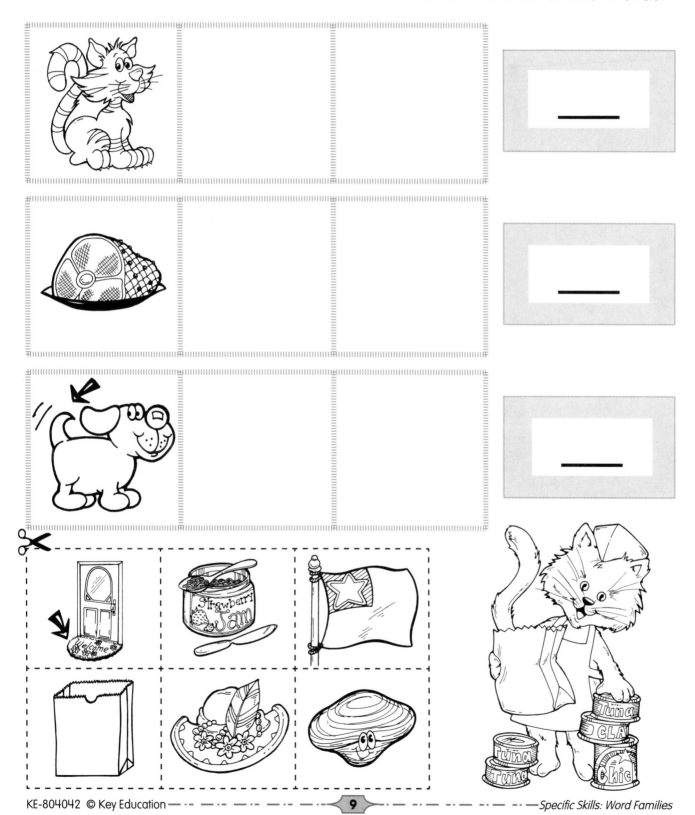

9 *Specific Skills: Word Families*

Write -an, -ap, and -at Words

Directions: Name each picture. Write the word in the boxes.

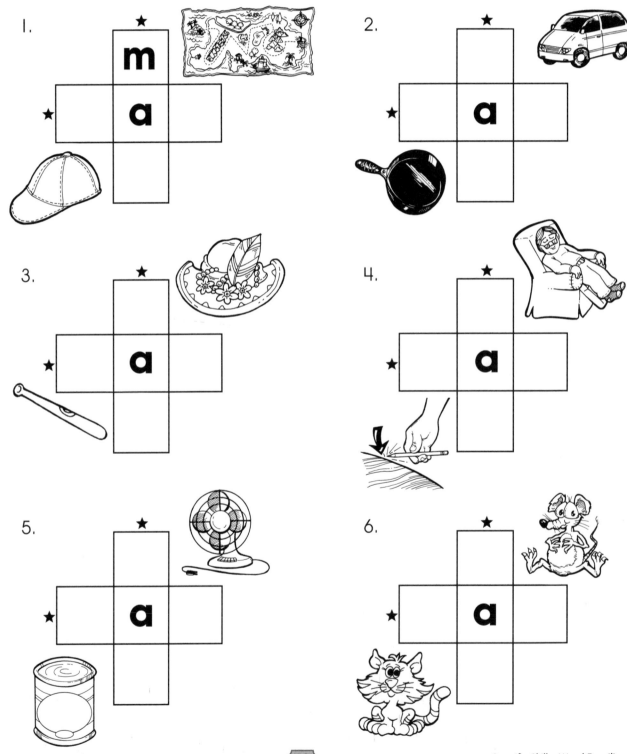

The -et Word Family

Directions: Circle each picture whose name rhymes with **pet**.

pet

Something to Try! Write three words that rhyme with **pet**.

net _____ _____

More Short "e" Word Families

Directions: Cut out the pictures below. Glue the pictures that rhyme in the same row. Write the letter for the sound at the **end** of the words.

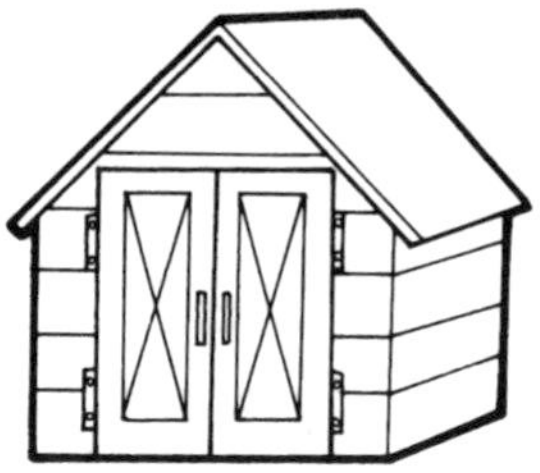

___

___

Something to Try!
Write three words that rhyme with **shed**.

red _____ _____

Write three words that rhyme with **pen**.

men _____ _____

Write -ed, -en, and -et Words

Directions: Name each picture. Write the word in the boxes.

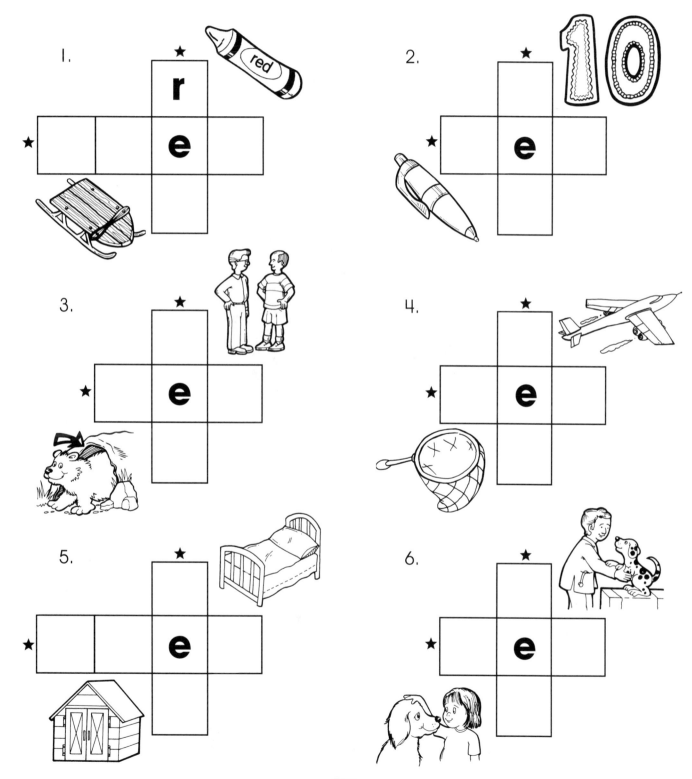

1. ★   r

   ★   e

2. ★

   ★   e

3. ★

   ★   e

4. ★

   ★   e

5. ★

   ★   e

6. ★

   ★   e

The -ig Word Family

Directions: Draw a line from the word **pig** to each picture whose name rhymes.

pig

  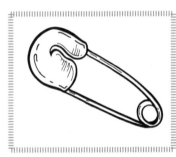

Something to Try! Cut out the pictures above. Sort them into groups. Glue the pictures on another sheet of paper. Label each group.

More Short "i" Word Families

Directions: Name each picture in each row. Write the letter for the sound at the **end** of the words.

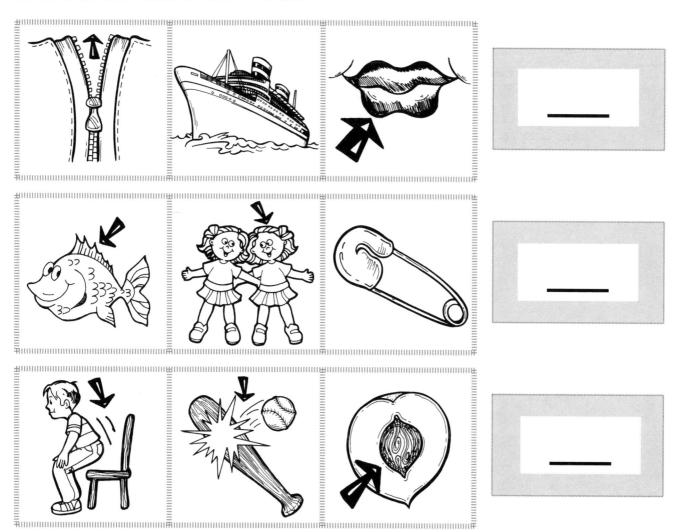

Something to Try! Read the words. Draw lines to match the words that rhyme.

zip   win

pit   lip

fin   sit

Write -ig, -in, -ip, and -it Words

Directions: Name each picture. Write the word in the boxes.

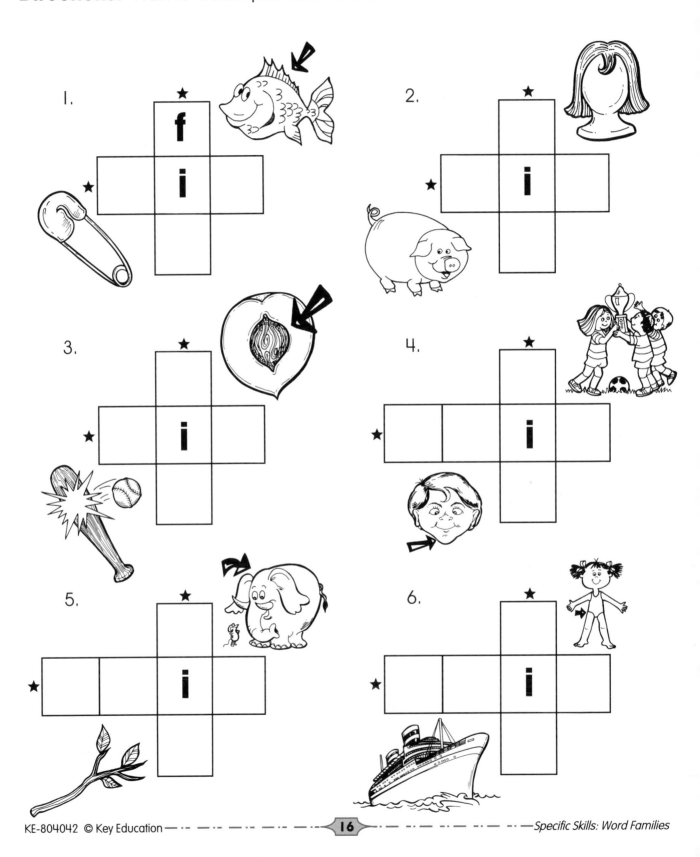

The -ot Word Family

Directions: Draw a line from the **robot** to each picture whose name rhymes with **pot**.

Something to Try! Cut out the letters. Make words that rhyme with **pot**. Write the words below.

_____

_____

_____

_____

l	r
t d	p s
o t d	h p s
o	h

More Short "o" Word Families

Directions: Cut out the pictures below. Glue the pictures that rhyme in the same row. Write the letter for the sound at the **end** of the words.

Write -ob, -og, -op, -ot, and -ox Words

Directions: Name each picture. Write the word in the boxes.

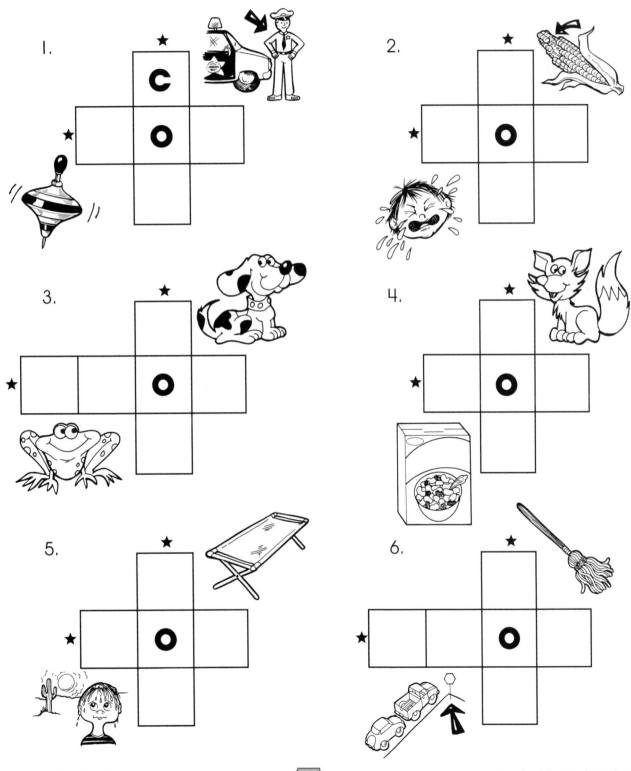

The -*ug* Word Family

Directions: Draw a line from the word **dug** to each picture whose name rhymes.

 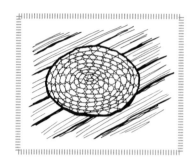 

dug

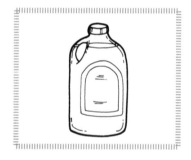 

Something to Try! Cut out the pictures above. Sort them into groups. Glue the pictures on another sheet of paper. Label each group.

More Short "u" Word Families

Directions: Cut out the pictures below. Glue the pictures that rhyme in the same row. Write the letter for the sound at the **end** of the words.

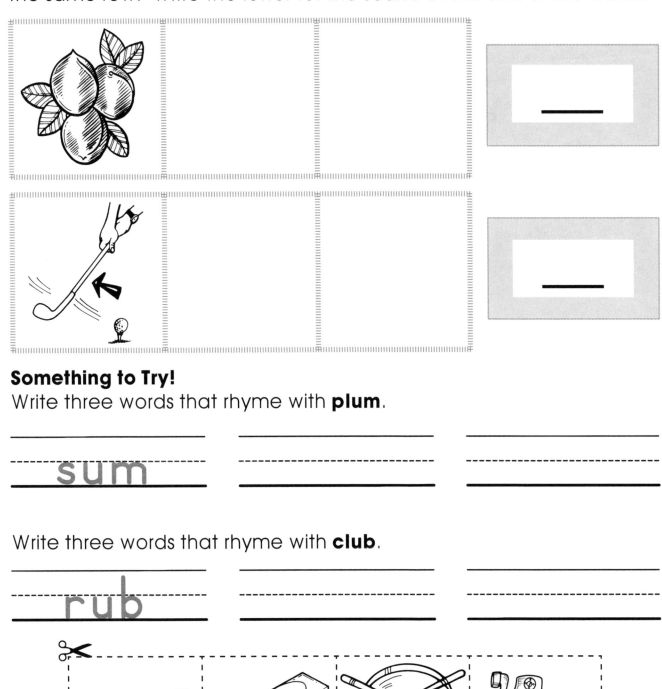

Something to Try!

Write three words that rhyme with **plum**.

___sum___   _____   _____

Write three words that rhyme with **club**.

___rub___   _____   _____

Write -*ub*, -*ug*, -*um*, and -*ut* Words

Directions: Name each picture. Write the word in the boxes.

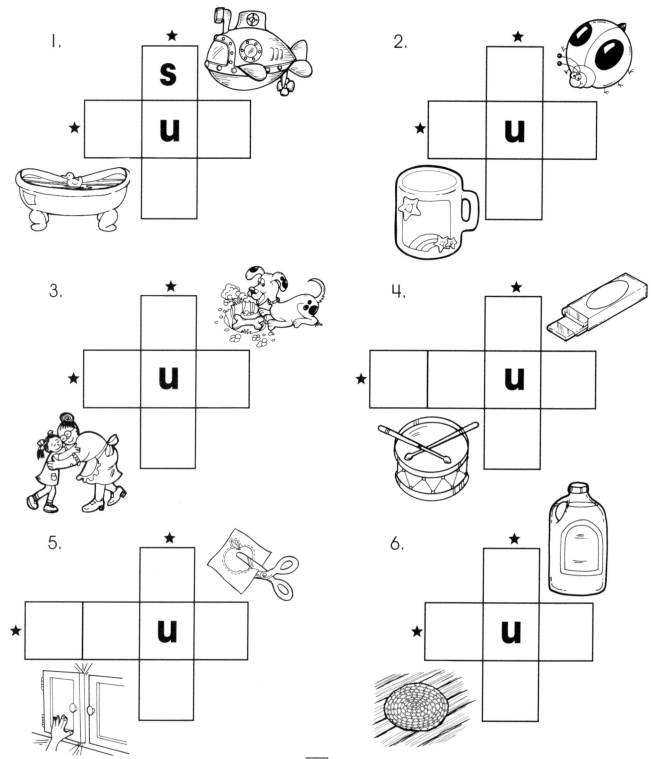

Say and Match: *-ap*, *-at*, and *-op* Words

To the Teacher: Copy the leaves below and the Say and Match Game mat on page 24 onto colorful card stock. Cut out the leaves along the dashed lines. Have students say the name of each picture on the game mat and then place the leaf with the corresponding word family on the picture.

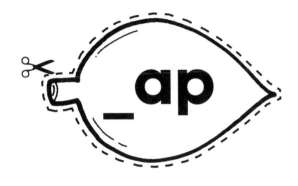

Say and Match Game

(Directions are found on page 23.)

Read and Race!

Getting Ready: Make two copies of pages 25 and 26 and one copy of pages 27 and 28 on colorful card stock for each group of three players. Cut out the game cards along the dashed lines and trim page 27 as indicated. Overlap page 27 on page 28 to make the game board and then glue the scene to the inside panels of a file folder. Provide game markers for the players.

To Play the Game: Shuffle the game cards and then place them facedown in a stack near the game board. First, determine which player begins the game. Have players take turns drawing one card and then saying the name of the picture aloud. The player then moves his game marker to the nearest corresponding phonogram (word part) and then places the card faceup in the discard pile. If the player's choice is incorrect, the player returns the game marker to the previous space on which it was resting. The first player to land on the last space on the path ("Finish") is the winner.

Alternatively, provide players with a standard die, pencil, and paper instead of the game cards. Have players take turns rolling the die and then moving their game markers the corresponding number of spaces on the game path. For each turn when a player's game marker lands on a phonogram, the player uses that word part to write a word. (Some spaces on the path feature two phonograms that can be used in words.) When all players reach the "Finish" space, have them compare their words and award one point for each word that appears on only one list. The player who earns the most points wins the game.

Draw 2 cards. **Draw 2 cards.** **Draw 2 cards.**

(Directions are found on page 25.)

Read and

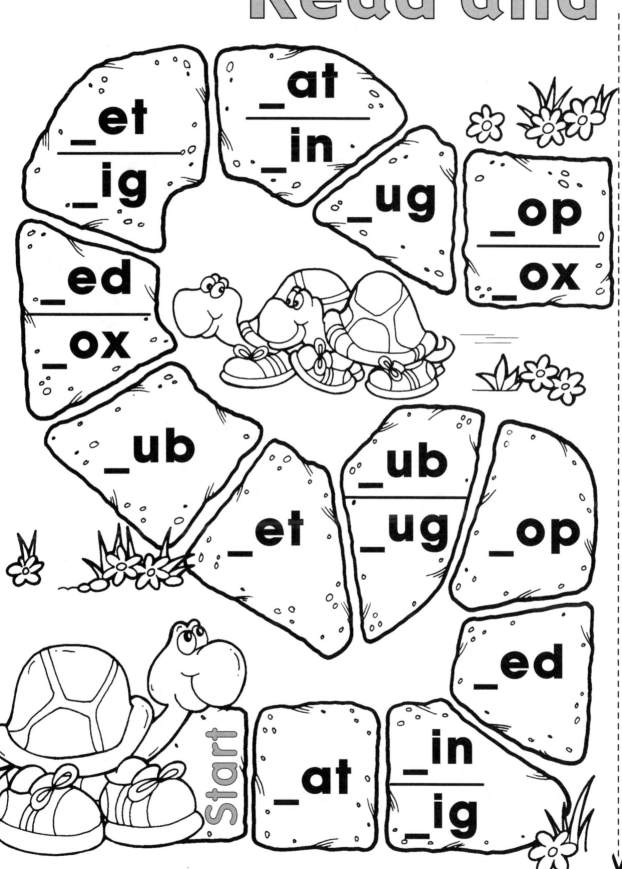

Race!

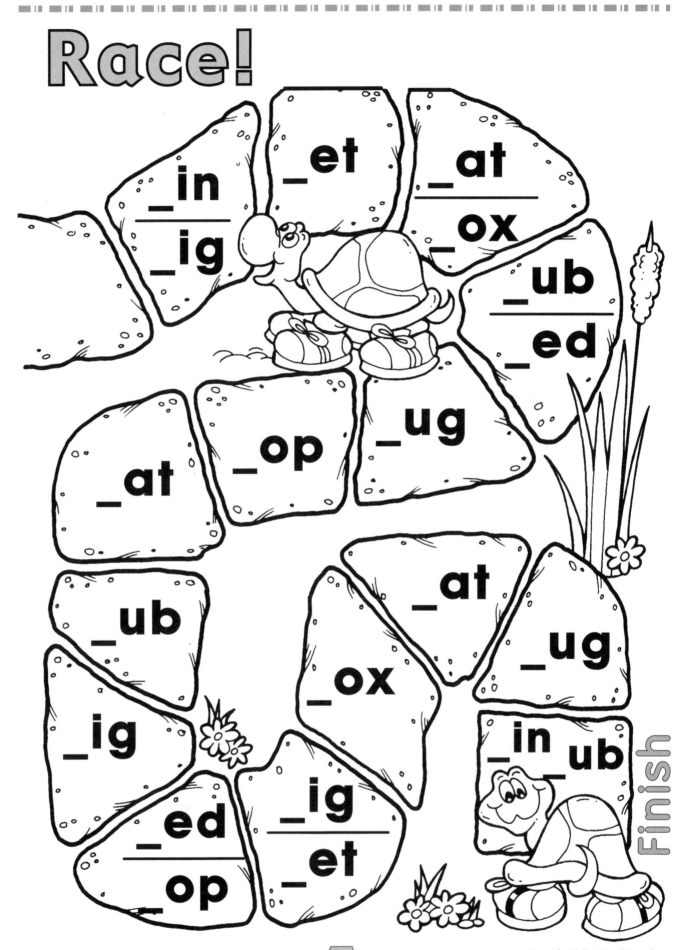

_in
_ig

_et

_at
ox

_ub
_ed

_at

_op

_ug

_ub

_ig

_ed
_op

_ig
_et

_ox

_at

_ug

_in ub
_

Finish

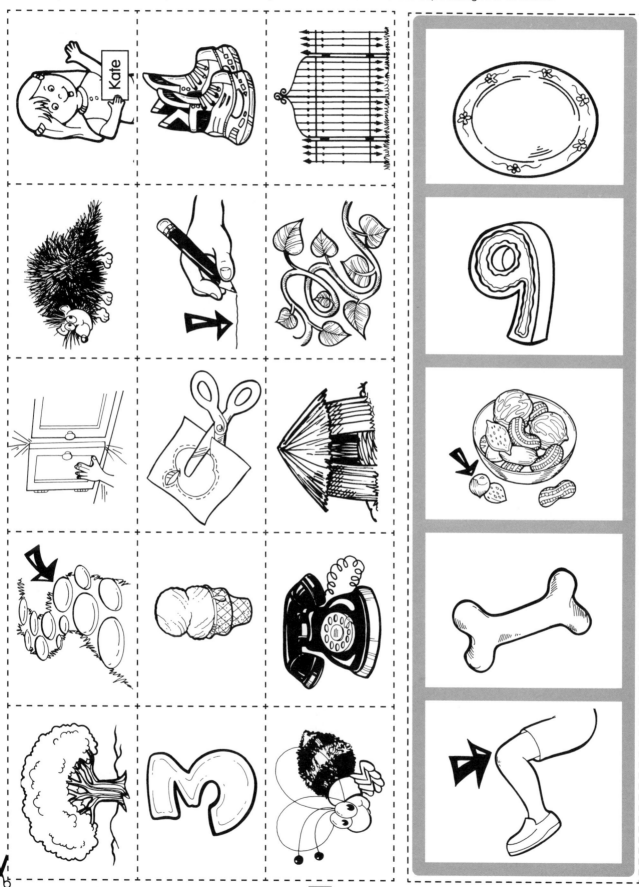

29

Rhyme to Match

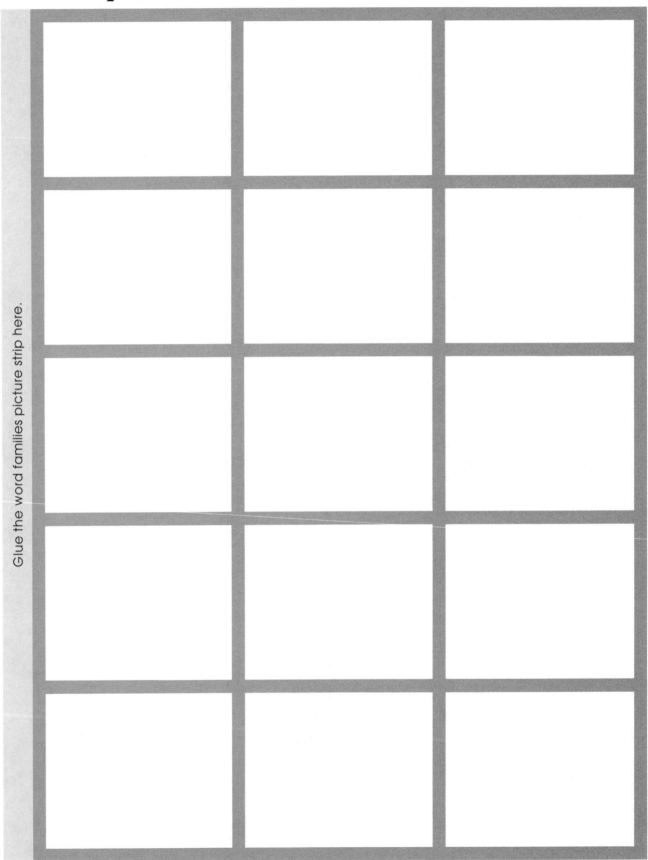

Glue the word families picture strip here.

The -*ain* Word Family

Directions: Draw a line from the large **A** to each picture whose name rhymes with **train**.

train

A

Something to Try! Write three words that rhyme with **train**.

chain _____   _____   _____

31

Find the Word Family

Directions: Cut out the pictures below. Name the pictures and glue them in the correct word families.

_ane	_ake	_an	_ail	_ace

32

The -ee Word Family

Directions: Draw a line from the large **E** to each picture whose name rhymes with **see**.

see

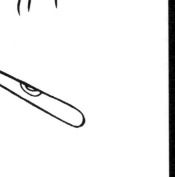

Something to Try! Write three words that rhyme with **see**.

three _____   _____   _____

The -eep, -eet, and -ent Families

To the Teacher: Read aloud the directions and have the child draw pictures in the boxes.

Draw **sheep** riding in a **jeep**.

Draw two **sheep** going to **sleep**.

Draw two **feet** walking down the **street**.

Draw how two friends **meet** and **greet**.

Draw **Kent** spending I **cent**.

Draw a **tent** that is **bent**.

The -ice and -ike Word Families

Directions: Draw a line from the large **I** to each picture whose name rhymes with either **Mike** or **mice**.

mice

Mike

Something to Try! Write three words that rhyme with **Mike.**

hike _____ _____ _____

Write three words that rhyme with **mice.**

slice _____ _____ _____

Specific Skills: Word Families

Find the Word Family

Directions: Cut out the pictures below. Name the pictures and glue them in the correct word families.

_ive	_ell	_ick	_un	_ine

Name_____ Date_____

The -ose and -one Word Families

Directions: Draw a line from the large **O** to each picture whose name rhymes with either **nose** or **stone**.

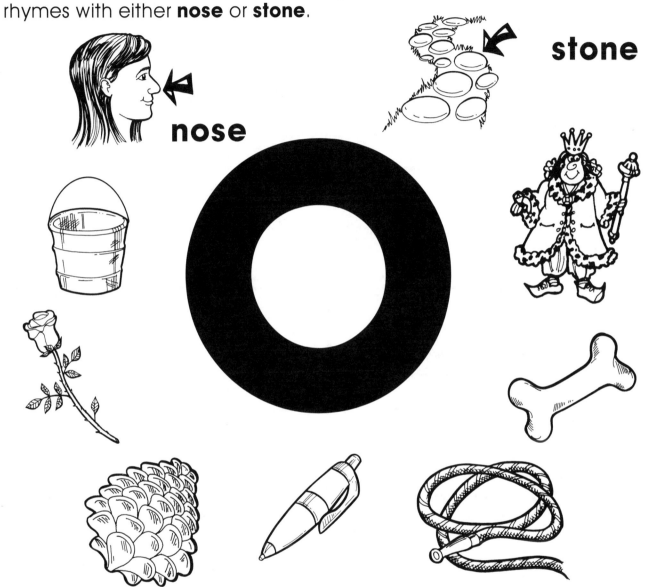

nose

stone

Something to Try! Write three words that rhyme with **nose**.

__pose__ _____ _____

Write three words that rhyme with **bone**.

__stone__ _____ _____

Fill In the Names

Directions: Name each picture. Write the word in the box by the picture. In the **Word Family Bank**, draw an **X** in each box when it is used.

bl ____	r ____
gl ____	c ____
b ____	f ____
h ____	m ____
g ____	sn ____

Word Family Bank

_oat	_ow	_op	_oat	_ow
_ow	_oat	_ow	_obe	_ox

Looking for Clues

Directions: Say the name of each picture. Write the missing letters for each word.

tu____   pr____

____m   J____

fl____   tu____

____c

Building -*une* and -*ute* Words

Directions: Name each picture. Use the letters in the blocks to write each word. Color each block as the letter is used.

_ _ _ _   _ _ _ _   _ _ _ _ _   _ _ _ _

Directions: Write words from the **Word Bank** on the lines.

Word Bank

cute	prune
flute	tune
June	

Playing a Tune in June

Kay looked so __ __ __ __ playing her flute.

Her mother told her, "Please play

a __ __ __ __ every day in __ __ __ __!"

Kay played and played her __ __ __ __ __ so much,

her mouth dried up like a __ __ __ __ __ .

More Fill In the Names

Directions: Name each picture. Write the word in the box by the picture. Draw an **X** in each box in the **Word Family Bank** when it is used.

h _____	h _____
t _____	c _____
f _____	r _____
sm _____	r _____
m _____	sh _____

Word Family Bank

_ish	_eep	_ule	_oke	_oad
_ole	_ill	_oad	_ain	_ube

Match 'Em Up!

Directions: Read each sentence and name the picture. Write the correct word from the **Word Bank** on the line.

Word Bank

brick	game	jet	ring	tent
cake	grapes	king	sun	

1. Can we make a _____?

2. Kammy lives in a  _____ house.

3. Did you see the  _____ fly over the lake?

4. Is the _____ high in the sky?

5. The girls are sleeping in the 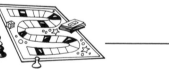 _____ .

6. Dad said, "Let's play a  _____ ."

7. Do you like to eat _____ ?

8. Give the _____ to the  _____ .

The -all Family Story

Directions: Read the story about the -all family. Use the **Letter Box** to write the missing letters on the lines.

Letter Box

b	h	m	sm	t	w

Let's meet the -all family. Dad is very __ **a l l** .

He holds the baby girl. She is very __ __ **a l l** .

Mom cleans the __ **a l l** because

the cat scratched the __ **a l l** .

Susan, the big sister,  goes to the __ **a l l** after

she takes her little brother to play  __ **a l l** .

Directions: Can y'all think of any other -all words? If so, write them on the lines.

_____   _____   _____

---------------   ---------------   ---------------

_____   _____   _____

The -*ug* Word Family Puzzle

Directions: Name each picture. Write the word on the lines. Then, print the word in the puzzle. Each word rhymes with **mug**.

Across

  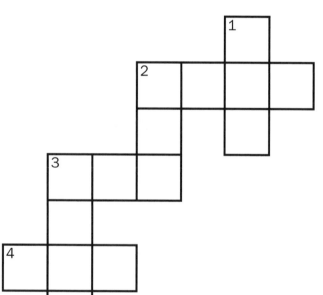

2. ___ ___ ___ ___   3. ___ ___ ___   4. ___ ___ ___

Down

1. ___ ___ ___

2. ___ ___ ___

3. ___ ___ ___ ___

The -ack Family Story

Directions: Read the story about the *-ack* family. Write the correct words from the **Word Bank** on the lines. Some words may be used more than once.

Word Bank

backpack	Mack	stack
black	quack	track
crack	sack	
Jack	snack	

Jack has a friend named __ __ __ __ .

At school, their pet duck likes to __ __ __ __ __ .

__ __ __ __ __ and __ __ __ __ each

have a __ __ __ __ __ __ __ __ __ .

In each backpack are a __ __ __ __ __ __

and a __ __ __ __ __ __ __ __ __ __ .

Each day before school, the boys place all

of the storybooks in a large, neat __ __ __ __ __ .

They give the duck some __ __ __ __ __ ed corn

as a special __ __ __ __ __ __ . Sometimes,

the toy train must be put back on its __ __ __ __ __ .

More Match 'Em Up!

Directions: Read each sentence and name the picture. Write the correct word from the **Word Bank** on the line.

Word Bank

car	fell	puck	stole	top
dish	pill	rake	sub	

1. Mom said, "Please _____ the leaves."

2. When I was sick, I had to take a  _____ .

3. My baby brother really likes his _____ .

4. Jim plays with his _____ in the tub.

5. My big sister has a new  _____ .

6. Lee slipped and _____ on the ice.

7. Please fill my _____ with ice cream.

8. My friend Tommy  _____ second base.

9. When I play hockey, I try to hit the  _____ .

The -eet Word Family

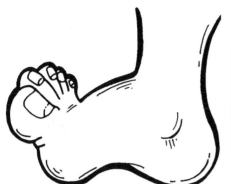

Word Bank

meet	sweet
tweet	greet
Street	feet

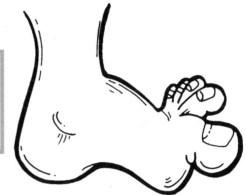

Directions: Write the correct words from the **Word Bank** on the lines. One word will be used twice.

1. There are two big __ __ __ __ at the top of this page.

2. Mother said, "Please __ __ __ __ __ your grandmother at the door."

3. Who lives on Peachtree __ __ __ __ __ __ ?

4. John was very excited to __ __ __ __ his teacher.

5. The cookies were chocolate and very __ __ __ __ __ .

6. The little bird said, " __ __ __ __ __ , __ __ __ __ __ !"

Something to Try! Write the Word Bank words in **ABC** order.

1. _____   4. _____

2. _____   5. _____

3. _____   6. _____

Name_____   Date _____

The *-ice* Word Family

Directions: Name each picture. Circle the correct beginning letter or letters of the name. Write the word. Use it to complete a sentence.

l b (r)	pl sl m	d f pr
 rice		
_____	_____	_____

t pr w	m o y	l k sp

_____	_____	_____

1. The ___ ___ ___ ___ ___ of this baseball glove is too much!

2. He needs some ___ ___ ___ ___ ___ for his toast.

3. My sister wants more ___ ___ ___ ___ in her dish.

4. I would like a ___ ___ ___ ___ of cherry pie.

5. The teacher said, "Please roll the ___ ___ ___ ___ to start!"

6. The ___ ___ ___ ___ ate all of the cheese.

The -ose Word Family

Word Bank

those	noses
close	hose
rose	chose

Directions: Write the correct words from the **Word Bank** on the lines.

1. There are two big ___ ___ ___ ___ ___ at the top of this page.

2. Mother said, "Thank you for the beautiful ___ ___ ___ ___ ."

3. Brent ___ ___ ___ ___ ___ chocolate ice cream for his party.

4. Our teacher told us to plant ___ ___ ___ ___ ___ seeds in dirt.

5. My uncle Tony used a ___ ___ ___ ___ to water the grass.

6. Aunt Milly said, "Please ___ ___ ___ ___ ___ the door!"

Something to Try! Write the Word Bank words in **ABC** order.

1. _____   4. _____

2. _____   5. _____

3. _____   6. _____

The -ool Word Family

Directions: Name each picture. Circle the correct beginning letter or letters of the name. Write the word. Use it to complete a sentence.

d r (c) 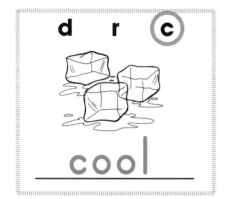 **cool**	g t h  _____	tr sch bl  _____
st wh cl 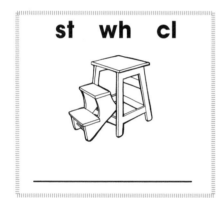 _____	p b v  _____	th br sp 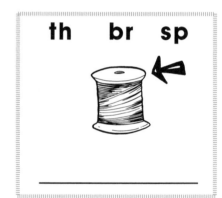 _____

1. I like to swim in a ___ ___ ___ ___ .

2. To reach the shelf, I have to stand on a ___ ___ ___ ___ ___.

3. Playing video games is really ___ ___ ___ ___ !

4. ___ ___ ___ ___ ___ ___ starts again at the end of summer.

5. Dad needs a ___ ___ ___ ___ to fix the deck.

6. Would you bring me a ___ ___ ___ ___ ___ of thread?

Sense or Nonsense?

Directions: Read each pair of sentences. Circle the sentence that makes sense. Draw a picture about that sentence.

1.

   A. Jack will be sleeping all night.

   B. Jack will be creeping all light.

2.

   A. Can you wap on the bloor?

   B. Can you tap on the door?

3.

   A. Oooh! I dropped my lum.

   B. Oooh! I dropped my gum.

4.

   A. Help! The goose is loose!

   B. Help! The moose is toose!

5.

   A. It will be fun to run in the sun on the beach.

   B. It will be fun to bun in the pun on the beach.

The -*ug* Family Story

Directions: Read the story about the -*ug* family. Write the missing letters from the **Letter Box** on the lines. One letter is used twice.

Let's meet the –*ug* family. Grandpa is feeling smug.

He knows who the  __ __ u g is

that took an old pot, a pan, and some  __ u g s !

Grandma gives him a __ u g

before filling his __ u g with coffee.

Then, he tells her the story. Their dog is a __ u g  .

It had  __ u g a big hole under their __ u g

to hide the 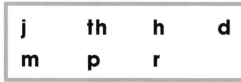 __ u g s .

Letter Box

j	th	h	d
m	p	r	

The -and Word Family

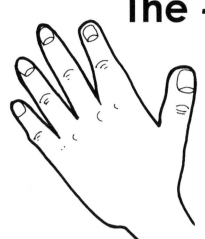
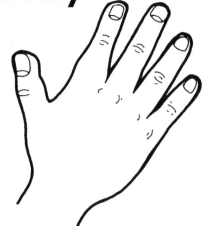

Word Bank

hands	band
stand	sand
land	brand

Directions: Write the correct words from the **Word Bank** on the lines.

1. There are two big __ __ __ __ __ at the top of this page.

2. We watched the __ __ __ __ during halftime.

3. At the beach, I built a castle out of __ __ __ __ .

4. Which __ __ __ __ __ of chips do you like best?

5. Mrs. Smith said, "Please __ __ __ __ __ by your desk."

6. My grandfather has a farm with lots of __ __ __ __ .

Something to Try! Write the Word Bank words in **ABC** order.

1. _____   4. _____

2. _____   5. _____

3. _____   6. _____

The -oy Word Family

Directions: Write the -oy words from the **Word Bank** on the lines.

Roy and His Toys

There is a _____ named _____.

He often jumps for _____.

He used a _____ to get lots of _____

so that he can pretend to be a _____.

Word Bank

boy	joy	Roy
cowboy	ploy	toys

Making Words

Directions: Name each picture. Use the letters on the blocks to write the word. Color each block as the letter is used.

The *-ip* Word Family

Directions: Name each picture. Circle the correct beginning letter or letters of the name. Write the word. Use it to complete a sentence.

pl   br   (sk)

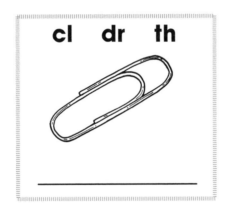

__skip__

s   k   r

_____

b   h   w

_____

ch   tr   sh

_____

cl   dr   th

_____

pr   cl   fl

_____

1. My mother uses a paper ___ ___ ___ ___ to keep the papers together.

2. My big sister likes to ___ ___ ___ ___ rope with her friends.

3. Before the game, the referee had to ___ ___ ___ ___ a coin.

4. My parents said, "We're going on a cruise ___ ___ ___ ___."

5. When LaTanya fell, she hurt her ___ ___ ___ .

6. I couldn't wait to take a ___ ___ ___ of my soda.

The -ick Family Story

Directions: Read the silly story about the -ick family. Write the correct words from the **Word Bank** on the lines below. Two words are used more than once.

Word Bank

brick	flick	Rick	thick
chick	Nick	sick	trick
Dick	Quick	stick	

Once upon a time, there were three brothers named

__ __ __ __ , __ __ __ __ , and __ __ __ __ __ .

They lived in a small __ __ __ __ __ house

with their pet chick .

When the pet __ __ __ __ __ got __ __ __ __ ,

the boys had a slick __ __ __ __ __ .

They would turn off the lights

and watch a __ __ __ __ __ .

Soon, the bird would be pecking at its food

and a __ __ __ __ __ __ __ __ __ __ .

One day, __ __ __ __ __ said, " __ __ __ __ __ !

Let's get a new pet __ __ __ __ __ ."

"No!" said the other boys. "We like this __ __ __ __ __ !"

Name_____   Date _____

More Sense or Nonsense?

Directions: Read each pair of sentences. Circle the sentence that makes sense. Draw a picture about that sentence.

1.
   A. I read a story about a white unicorn.
   B. I read a story about a bite tricorn.

2.
   A. I gave my teacher a waffy bapple.
   B. I gave my teacher a taffy apple.

3.
   A. Sometimes a sneeze can be very loud.
   B. Sometimes a wheeze can be very proud.

4.
   A. In our EP class, we can loot boops.
   B. In our PE class, we can shoot hoops.

Something to Try! Write two more sets of sense and nonsense sentences on the back of this paper. Give them to a friend to read.

The -eat Word Family Questions

Directions: Write the correct words from the **Word Bank** on the lines. Some words will be used twice.

1. Shouldn't you __ __ __ __ the __ __ __ __ to cook it?

2. If your shoes have __ __ __ __ __ __ on them, will they help you __ __ __ __ the other football team?

3. Is that a __ __ __ __ __ in your skirt?

4. Will it be __ __ __ __ to sit  in the front __ __ __ __ of the car?

5. Was he a cheat when he __ __ __ __ her to the front __ __ __ __ in the room?

6. Is that your goat making that loud __ __ __ __ __?

7. Do you think pizza  is a __ __ __ __ __ __ __ __ __?

Word Bank

beat	cleats	meat	pleat	treat
bleat	heat	neat	seat	

Something to Try! Find out some facts about wheat. Write down what you learn on the back of this paper.

The -*ip* Word Family Puzzle

Directions: Read each clue. Find the word in the **Word Bank**. Then, write the word in the puzzle.

Word Bank

blip
clip
flip
grip
lip
quip
rip
skip
slip
trip

Across
2. Worn under a dress
4. A tear
6. To toss a coin
8. You use two to smile
9. A joke

Down
1. To hold tightly
2. Slower than a run
3. To fall over something
5. A spot of light on a computer screen
7. Holds paper together

A Jumbo -*ing* Word Find

Directions: Read the words in the **Word Bank**. Look down and across for the words in the word find. Circle the 12 words.

a	g	f	i	m	q	t	v	g	n	r	g	b
b	i	t	h	i	n	g	x	s	w	n	d	r
f	g	n	b	j	m	a	s	t	k	h	r	i
l	z	h	c	o	q	d	g	r	j	c	z	n
i	f	y	a	x	n	t	z	i	t	f	k	g
n	m	u	j	t	q	g	w	n	h	d	j	y
g	w	v	z	p	n	h	t	g	l	v	a	r
w	m	g	i	j	s	k	c	l	i	n	g	i
t	s	l	n	q	h	i	f	u	f	s	f	o
i	p	j	g	v	j	n	z	a	s	i	n	g
y	r	i	w	p	x	g	n	t	p	c	r	k
a	i	g	g	z	k	f	m	r	d	v	i	y
c	n	x	w	i	n	g	x	i	b	w	g	i
u	g	s	u	o	w	r	p	n	o	n	u	m
c	p	x	l	s	t	i	n	g	n	n	g	n

Word Bank

bring	cling	fling	king
ring	sing	spring	sting
string	thing	wing	zing

To the Teacher: Copy the game board onto colorful card stock. Select words that students need to practice reading. Write the words on small index cards that have been cut in half. Taking turns, each player draws and reads aloud a word card. If the word is read correctly, the player rolls a die and moves the game marker the corresponding number of spaces on the path. The first player to reach the end of the path is the winner.

Answer Key

Page 6 – Pretest/Posttest
bug, hit, fan, jet, pig, dot, cat, fox

Page 7 – Pretest/Posttest
pool, hole, drum, cube, snake, bed, king, face, rose, feet

Page 8
Circled: fan, pan, can, van
Bottom of page: Answers will vary.

Page 9
Row 1: hat, mat, t; Row 2: clam, jam, m; Row 3: flag, bag, g

Page 10
1. map, cap; 2. van, pan; 3. hat, bat; 4. nap, tap; 5. fan, can; 6. rat, cat

Page 11
Circled: jet, vet, net
Bottom of page: Answers will vary.

Page 12
Row 1: bed, sled, d; Row 2: ten, men, n
Bottom of page: Answers will vary.

Page 13
1. red, sled; 2. ten, pen; 3. men, den; 4. jet, net; 5. bed, shed; 6. vet, pet

Page 14
Matched: fig, wig, twig, dig, jig, big
Bottom of page: Answers will vary.

Page 15
Row 1: p; Row 2: n; Row 3: t;
Bottom of page: zip, lip; pit, sit; fin, win

Page 16
1. fin, pin; 2. wig, pig; 3. pit, hit; 4. win, chin; 5. big, twig; 6. hip, ship

Page 17
Matched: pot, cot, knot, hot, dot
Bottom of page: Answers will vary.

Page 18
Row 1: mop, top, p; Row 2: dog, log, g; Row 3: box, fox, x

Page 19
1. cop, top; 2. cob, sob; 3. dog, frog; 4. fox, box; 5. cot, hot; 6. mop, stop

Page 20
Matched: rug, hug, mug, jug, bug
Bottom of page: Answers will vary.

Page 21
Row 1: gum, drum, m; Row 2: tub, sub, b
Bottom of page: Answers will vary.

Page 22
1. sub, tub; 2. bug, mug; 3. dug, hug; 4. gum, drum; 5. cut, shut; 6. jug, rug

Page 24
_ap: cap, clap; _at: bat, cat, mat; _op: drop, hop, stop

Pages 25–28
(Possible matches) _at: bat, cat, hat, mat; _ed: bed, shed, sled; _et: jet, pet, vet; _ig: dig, pig, wig; _in: fin, pin, twin; _op: cop, mop, top; _ox: box, fox; _ub: cub, club, sub, tub; _ug: bug, hug, mug, rug

Page 29–30
Matched: plate—Kate, gate, skate; nine—line, porcupine, vine; nut—cut, hut, shut; bone—cone, phone, stone; knee—bee, three, tree

Page 31
Matched: rain, drain, brain
Bottom of page: Answers will vary.

Page 32
_ane: crane, plane, cane; _ake: snake, rake, cake; _an: van, fan, pan; _ail: sail, tail, snail; _ace: brace, face, race

Page 33
Matched: three, knee, tree, bee
Bottom of page: Answers will vary.

Page 34
Answers will vary.

Page 35
Matched: dice, rice, bike, hike, spike
Bottom of page: Answers will vary.

Page 36
_ive: five, hive, dive; _ell: shell, bell, well; _ick: brick, kick, stick; _un: bun, sun, run; _ine: vine, nine, pine (tree)

Page 37
Matched: bone, hose, pinecone, rose
Bottom of page: Answers will vary.

Answer Key

Page 38
blow, row, globe, coat, boat, fox, hop, mow, goat, snow

Page 39
tune, prune, mule, June, flute, tube, cube

Page 40
flute, tune, prune, June
Bottom of page: cute, tune, June, flute, prune

Page 41
hole, hill, toad, cube, fish, road, smoke, rain, mule, sheep

Page 42
1. cake, 2. brick, 3. jet, 4. sun, 5. tent, 6. game, 7. grapes, 8. ring, king

Page 43
tall, small, hall, wall, mall, ball
Bottom of page: Answers will vary.

Page 44
Across: 2. plug, 3. dug, 4. tug
Down: 1. jug, 2. pug, 3. drug

Page 45
Mack, quack, Jack, Mack, backpack, snack, black sack, stack, crack, snack, track

Page 46
1. rake, 2. pill, 3. top, 4. sub, 5. car, 6. fell, 7. dish, 8. stole, 9. puck

Page 47
1. feet, 2. greet, 3. Street, 4. meet, 5. sweet, 6. tweet, tweet
Bottom of page: 1. feet, 2. greet, 3. meet, 4. Street, 5. sweet, 6. tweet

Page 48
sl—slice, d—dice, pr—price, m—mice, sp—spice
1. price, 2. spice, 3. rice, 4. slice, 5. dice, 6. mice

Page 49
1. noses, 2. rose, 3. chose, 4. those, 5. hose, 6. close
Bottom of page: 1. chose, 2. close, 3. hose, 4. noses, 5. rose, 6. those

Page 50
t—tool, sch—school, st—stool, p—pool, sp—spool
1. pool, 2. stool, 3. cool, 4. School, 5. tool, 6. spool

Page 51
1. A., 2. B., 3. B., 4. A., 5. A

Page 52
thug, jugs, hug, mug, pug, dug, rug, jugs

Page 53
1. hands, 2. band, 3. sand, 4. brand, 5. stand, 6. land
Bottom of page: 1. band, 2. brand, 3. hands, 4. land, 5. sand, 6. stand

Page 54
boy, Roy, joy, ploy, toys, cowboy
Bottom of page: Roy, joy, boy, toy

Page 55
s—sip, h—hip, sh—ship, cl—clip, fl—flip
1. clip, 2. skip, 3. flip, 4. ship, 5. hip, 6. sip

Page 56
Dick, Nick, Rick, brick, chick, sick, trick, flick, thick stick, Nick, Quick, chick, chick

Page 57
1. A., 2. B., 3. A., 4. B.
Bottom of page: Answers will vary.

Page 58
1. heat, meat; 2. cleats, beat; 3. pleat; 4. neat, seat; 5. beat, seat; 6. bleat; 7. neat treat
Bottom of page: Answers will vary.

Page 59
Across: 2. slip, 4. rip, 6. flip, 8. lip, 9. quip
Down: 1. grip, 2. skip, 3. trip, 5. blip, 7. clip

Page 60
Check student's work.

Correlations to NCTE/IRA Standards and NAEYC/IRA Position Statement

Specific Skills: Word Families supports the NCTE/IRA *Standards for the English Language Arts* and the recommended teaching practices outlined in the NAEYC/IRA position statement *Learning to Read and Write: Developmentally Appropriate Practices for Young Children*.

NCTE/IRA *Standards for the English Language Arts*

Each activity in this book supports one or more of the following standards:

1. **Students read many different types of print and nonprint texts for a variety of purposes.**
   Students read pictures, letters, words, and sentences in order to do the activities in *Word Families*.

2. **Students use a variety of strategies to build meaning while reading.**
   The activities in *Word Families* support reading strategies such as word family and word recognition, phonemic awareness, letter-sound correspondence, and classification.

3. **Students communicate in spoken, written, and visual form, for a variety of purposes and a variety of audiences.**
   Activities in *Word Families* incorporate visual communication through drawing and cut-and-paste activities and writing through a wide variety of written activities.

4. **Students conduct research on a variety of topics and present their research findings in ways appropriate to their purpose and audience.**
   One activity in *Word Families* requires students to conduct research and present the information they find in writing.

NAEYC/IRA Position Statement *Learning to Read and Write: Developmentally Appropriate Practices for Young Children*

Each activity in this book supports one or more of the following recommended teaching practices for kindergarten and primary-grade students:

1. **Teachers read to children daily and provide opportunities for students to read independently both fiction and nonfiction texts.**
   Word Families includes a list of read-aloud picture books that support learning about rhymes and word families.

2. **Teachers provide opportunities for students to write many different kinds of texts for different purposes.**
   When completing the activities in *Word Families*, students write letters, words, and sentences to show what they have learned.

3. **Teachers provide writing experiences that allow children to develop from the use of nonconventional writing forms to more conventional forms.**
   While working through the activities in *Word Families*, students move from writing letters and filling in blanks to composing their own sentences.

4. **Teachers provide opportunities for children to work in small groups.**
   Word Families includes several games that are designed for small groups.

5. **Teachers provide challenging instruction that expands children's knowledge of their world and expands their vocabularies.**
   Word Families introduces many vocabulary words in different word families.

6. **Teachers adapt teaching strategies based on the individual needs of a child.**
   Word Families is designed specifically for students who may be working below grade level, so it is a great resource for teachers to meet individual student needs.